Books by Kenneth Koch

ONE TRAIN

KENNETH KOCH

Alfred A. Knopf   New York   1994

ONE TRAIN

POEMS

Some of these poems originally appeared in magazines as follows: "One Train," *New York Review of Books;* "At the Opera," *Poetry Project Newsletter;* "A Time Zone" *and* "On Aesthetics," *Paris Review;* "Io," *Artes;* "The First Step," *Grand Street;* "No One Else," *Princeton Library Journal;* "Poems by Ships at Sea," *The New Yorker;* "Talking to Patrizia," *Poetry* and "A New Guide," *American Poetry Review.* "Io" was written for the collection *After Ovid,* edited by James Lasdun and Michael Hofmann, to be published by Faber & Faber Ltd (England) and Farrar, Straus & Giroux (U.S.A.). "Energy in Sweden" was the text of a book made in collaboration with the French artist Bertrand Dorny.

Library of Congress Cataloging-in-Publication Data

Koch, Kenneth
   One train : poems / Kenneth Koch. — 1st ed.
      p.   cm.
   ISBN 0-679-43417-8
   I. Title.
PS3521.027055 1994   94-12088
811'.54—dc20   CIP

I thank JORDAN DAVIS for the (considerable) assistance he gave me with this book.

TO KAREN

CONTENTS

ONE TRAIN

One Train May Hide Another

(sign at a railroad crossing in Kenya)

In a poem, one line may hide another line,
As at a crossing, one train may hide another train.
That is, if you are waiting to cross
The tracks, wait to do it for one moment at
Least after the first train is gone. And so when you read
Wait until you have read the next line—
Then it is safe to go on reading.
In a family one sister may conceal another,
So, when you are courting, it's best to have them all in view
Otherwise in coming to find one you may love another.
One father or one brother may hide the man,
If you are a woman, whom you have been waiting to love.
So always standing in front of something the other
As words stand in front of objects, feelings, and ideas.
One wish may hide another. And one person's reputation may hide
The reputation of another. One dog may conceal another
On a lawn, so if you escape the first one you're not necessarily safe;
One lilac may hide another and then a lot of lilacs and on the Appia Antica
      one tomb
May hide a number of other tombs. In love, one reproach may hide another,
One small complaint may hide a great one.
One injustice may hide another—one colonial may hide another,
One blaring red uniform another, and another, a whole column. One bath
      may hide another bath
As when, after bathing, one walks out into the rain.
One idea may hide another: Life is simple
Hide Life is incredibly complex, as in the prose of Gertrude Stein
One sentence hides another and is another as well. And in the laboratory
One invention may hide another invention,
One evening may hide another, one shadow, a nest of shadows.
One dark red, or one blue, or one purple—this is a painting
By someone after Matisse. One waits at the tracks until they pass,
These hidden doubles or, sometimes, likenesses. One identical twin
May hide the other. And there may be even more in there! The obstetrician
Gazes at the Valley of the Var. We used to live there, my wife and I, but

3

One life hid another life. And now she is gone and I am here.
A vivacious mother hides a gawky daughter. The daughter hides
Her own vivacious daughter in turn. They are in
A railway station and the daughter is holding a bag
Bigger than her mother's bag and successfully hides it.
In offering to pick up the daughter's bag one finds oneself confronted by the mother's
And has to carry that one, too. So one hitchhiker
May deliberately hide another and one cup of coffee
Another, too, until one is over-excited. One love may hide another love or the same love
As when "I love you" suddenly rings false and one discovers
The better love lingering behind, as when "I'm full of doubts"
Hides "I'm certain about something and it is that"
And one dream may hide another as is well known, always, too. In the Garden of Eden
Adam and Eve may hide the real Adam and Eve.
Jerusalem may hide another Jerusalem.
When you come to something, stop to let it pass
So you can see what else is there. At home, no matter where,
Internal tracks pose dangers, too: one memory
Certainly hides another, that being what memory is all about,
The eternal reverse succession of contemplated entities. Reading *A Sentimental Journey* look around
When you have finished, for *Tristram Shandy,* to see
If it is standing there, it should be, stronger
And more profound and theretofore hidden as Santa Maria Maggiore
May be hidden by similar churches inside Rome. One sidewalk
May hide another, as when you're asleep there, and
One song hide another song; a pounding upstairs
Hide the beating of drums. One friend may hide another, you sit at the foot of a tree
With one and when you get up to leave there is another
Whom you'd have preferred to talk to all along. One teacher,
One doctor, one ecstasy, one illness, one woman, one man
May hide another. Pause to let the first one pass.
You think, Now it is safe to cross and you are hit by the next one. It can be important
To have waited at least a moment to see what was already there.

Passing Time in Skansen

I went dancing in Stockholm at a public dancing place
Out-of-doors. It was a beautiful summer evening,
Summer as it could only come in Sweden in nineteen-fifty.
You had to be young to go there.
Or maybe you could be old. But I didn't even see old people then.
Humanity was divided into male and female, American and other, students
    and nonstudents, etcetera.
The only thing that I could say in Swedish
Was "Yog talar endast svenska"
Which meant I speak only Swedish, whereas I thought it meant
I DON'T speak Swedish.
So the young ladies, delighted, talked to me very fast
At which I smiled and understood nothing,
Though sometimes I would repeat
Yog talar endast svenska.
The evening ended, my part of it did, when they started to do folk dances.
I didn't even know how to look at them, though I tried to for a while.
It was still light out though it was after eleven p.m.
I got on some kind of streetcar that eventually stopped near my hotel.

Energy in Sweden

Those were the days
When there was so much energy in and around me
I could take it off and put it back on, like clothes
That one has bought only for a ski trip
But then finds that one is using every day
Because every day is like a ski trip—
I think that's how I was at twenty-three.

Seeing those six young women in a boat I was on a ski trip.
They said, We are all from Minneapolis. This was in Stockholm.
The melding of American and Swedish-American female looks was a ski trip
Although I had no particular reason at that time to put all my energy on
Yet there it was, I had it, the way a giant has the hegemony of his nerves
In case he needs it, or the way a fisherman has all his poles and lines and
     lures, and a scholar all his books
The way a water heater has all its gas
Whether it is being used or not, I had all that energy.
Really, are you all from Minneapolis? I said, almost bursting with force.
And yes, one of them, about the second prettiest, replied. We are here for
     several days.

I thought about this moment from time to time
For eight or ten years. It seemed to me I should have done something at the
     time,
To have used all that energy. Lovemaking is one way to use it and writing is
     another.
Both maybe are overestimated, because the relation is so clear.
But that is probably human destiny and I'm not going to go against it here.
Sometimes there are the persons and not the energy, sometimes the energy
     and not the persons.
When the gods give both, a man shouldn't complain.

A New Guide

What is needed is a guide to all situations and places . . .
LE VICOMTE DE CYRILLAC

*Vous voyez cette ligne télégraphique au fond de la vallée
et dont le tracé rectiligne carpe la forêt sur la montagne
d'en face/ Tous les poteaux en sont de fer . . .*
BLAISE CENDRARS, *Feuilles de Route*

1

Look at this Champagne factory
It is in Epernay
From it comes dry white wine with innumerable bubbles
(It is made in a series of fifteen gabled white buildings—sheds)
Borges writes that mirrors and fornication are "abominable"
Because they increase the amount of reality
This champagne factory transforms reality rather than simply increasing it
Without it Epernay champagne wouldn't exist.

2

Look at this wolf.
He is lighter than a a car
But heavier than a baby carriage.
He is highly effective.
Each wolf manifestation is done entirely in the classic manner of a wolf.
He stands completely still.
He is not "too busy to talk to you,"
Not "in conference" or "on the phone."
Some day there may not be any more wolves.
Civilization has not been moving in a way that is favorable to them.
Meanwhile, there is this one.

3

Look at this opera.
People are moving without plan.
They are badly directed.
But how they can sing!
One can tell from the faces of the audience how marvelously they sing.
That man there's face is like a burst of diamonds.
That very slim woman has fallen in a faint.
Four nights ago at this opera house a man died.
The opera stopped four young men came with a stretcher to carry
    him out.
I was told that when he was in the lobby a doctor pronounced him
    dead.
Look at the audience now. They are full of life.

4

Look at this camel.
A man unused to camels is trying to mount it.
The camel's driver motions for the camel to kneel down
On its front knees, which it does.
The man mounts it. The camel gallops away.
To qualify for his position the man must demonstrate his ability to
    ride a camel. He has failed.
Maybe he will be given another chance—if it is decided that this was
    a defective camel.
The worst thing that can happen is that he will be out of a job. He
    will not be shot.
The camel crouches down now in the sand,
Quiet, able, and at ease, with nothing about it defective.
If the camel were found to be defective, it would be shot.
That much of the old way still goes on.

5

The purple architecture runs all around the top of the Buddhist temple and
    then it is graduated into sculptured green, yellow, and pink strips.
Look at the young monk in a yellow and orange silk gown—he begins a
    prayerful journey up the four hundred and fifty steps.
Red blue white and purple sculptured kings and demons and Buddhas look
    down at him as he climbs and then look level at him but never look up
    at him
For they are near the top and their heads aren't constructed so that they are
    able to bend.

6

Look at this orange.
It was "made" by that orange tree over there.
That orange tree seems to be smiling
As it waves a little bit, just the slightest little bit, in this Andalusian wind.
If it waved much more it might start to lose its oranges.
It would.

7

Look at this arch.
It is part of a building more than seven hundred years old.
Every day from the time he was eighteen, probably, the man who made it
    worked in stone.
Sometimes he had a day off—the stone would be in his mind.
He would find in his mind ideas for patterns, lines, and angels.
Now those ideas are gone.
We have a different art.
But for what we believe most we don't have art at all.

8

The woman is covered by a sheet and the man has on a white mask.
The man takes out the woman's heart
And puts in another. He bends down to listen—
The new heart is beating! He asks for the wound to be closed.
He takes off his mask and goes into another room.
The woman stays in this room. She has a good chance of staying alive.

9

Look at this old tower in Lisbon that is now a museum for Portuguese blue
    tiles called Azulejos.
On each tile is a patterning of blue lines,
Thick ones and thin ones curving and straight but more curved ones than
    straight ones
And on most of them a picture and on some of them, actually on a good
    many of them, words.
One tells the story of Orpheus
On this one is a young woman
Holding a cane she points to an allegorical landscape—
A river, a bridge, and sheep. Underneath the image is written
WHATEVER PROSPERS, PROSPERS BEST IN ITS OWN PLACE.
This other tile (there are, it is said, eighty
Thousand of them, one cannot describe them all)
Shows a large blue-and-white-scaled fish. Underneath it, it says
In dark blue letters, in Latin, PISCIS NUNQUAM DORMET: THE
    FISH (or THIS FISH) NEVER SLEEPS.

10

You see this actor, on this stage, he is rehearsing his role in a play
Shakespeare's *A Winter's Tale*. He wears jeans and a frayed white shirt.
It is not yet dress rehearsal. He is rehearsing the part of Florizel. He is
    speaking
In unrhymed decasyllabic verse. Over here to his left is a young woman,
    Perdita.
She too is casually dressed—shirt and jeans.
Her brown hair is tied behind her head in a knot.

11

Look at this Greece.
It is hardly the same as ancient Greece at all
Not even the old buildings:
Look at this man walking with this woman
In a public park in Athens, in possession of happy lust.
Their faces can't have been the same in the fifth century BC.
Nothing can have been.

12

Look at this woman.
It has taken the human race millions of years for anyone to get to be the
    way she is:
An old woman in a red dress sitting looking at television.
Look at her hands.
They are a little dry but she is healthy.
She is eighty-two years old.
On the television screen is pictured a ship. There is a close-up of the deck,
    where
A little boy is playing with a dog. The woman laughs.

13

Look at the clouds.
They may be what I look at most of all
Without seeing anything.
It may be that many other things are the same way
But with clouds it's obvious.

The motorboat runs through the sky reflected in the river.
Look at the long trail of clouds behind.

14

Look at this celebration.
The people are festive, wearing masks.
There is a great variety of masks—dog mask, horse mask, mermaid mask,
     mask of a giant egg—
Many people are drinking despite the mask.
To get the drink to their lips they tilt the mask.
The masks, tilted upwards, look like hats.

15

Callé de los Espasmos

This is Spasms Street, named for a symptom of a fever one can get from
     mosquitoes at the very end of this street, where it becomes a path, near
     the mountain and surrounded by jungle, and leads to a waterfall and
     also sometimes to this fever.
Few people contract the disease and few know why the street is named
     Spasms Street. It is identified now and then by signposts: Calle de los
     Espasmos. The house this woman lives in is a kilometre from here, the
     zone is not dangerous.

16

Look at this bannister.
People put their hands on it as they went down.
Many many many many hands. Many many many many times.
It became known as the "Bannister of Ladies' Hands". It was said one could
    feel the smoothness of their hands when one touched it oneself.
Actually what one felt was the smoothness of the marble
That had been worn down by so many touching hands.
Look at the sign that is on it now: The Bannister of Ladies' Hands. To
    Preserve This Monument Each Person Is Requested To Touch
    It Only Once.
Look at the young boy there touching it twice, then a third time.
What if a guard catches him.
The fear is that if the bannister is touched too much it may completely wear
    away—the illusion of touching the soft hands of women in low-cut red
    dresses, going down to their friends and lovers, will exist no more.
The sensation will have vanished from the world.

17

Look at this beautiful road
On which horses have trodden
Centuries ago. Then it was a dirt road.
Now it is a stone road
Covered with tar.
The horses' prints are no longer visible.
Nothing is visible. Yes,
Now a motorcycle and a car go past.

18

Look at my friend.
He is saying to me Did you know that I am sixty-three?
He has a beautiful wrinkled face but in which the face has an almost
    complete mastery over the wrinkles. The wrinkling process is still held
    in abeyance by the face.
You're looking pretty good to me, I say.
He smiles.
Some day his face will be totally invaded by wrinkles like the pond in the
    Luxembourg Gardens on a windy fall day.
Even then, though, the main features of his face that I like will be visible.

19

This Egyptian temple is five thousand years old.
Look at the lion and look at the baboon. Both are in sphinx shape.
Look at the pattern of the notes on this sheet of music.
Look at this well-known beauty now seventy years old. She says
It's fine up till seventy when you can still be sexually appealing. But after
    that—
Look at the harbingers of tempest—or of spring?—birds,
Birds are like thoughts that the sky had after it had made its decision
About what to do, and today they are flying violently.
Look at this cloth
Spread out on the roof, beginning to show drops of rain.
Look at the green iris of this Peruvian flamingo's eye.
Look at the gravel on this path. Look at this old man's unevenly knitted
    grey sleeve.

20

Look at this woman.
The man she is with can't believe she has any connection to him.
She doesn't. She turns the corner.
But he walks after her.
After a few hundred feet he has the courage to say Hello.
You are very beautiful. May I walk with you a little ways.
She nods her head, smiling. She doesn't understand him because he is not
    speaking Spanish,
The only language she understands.
The man says, in English, I have just arrived in Barcelona.
She smiles, not understanding a word, except "Barcelona."
Two women and three men go by, speaking Catalan.

Io

Look at this lovely river maid, who bears the name of Io—
Her youthful beauty caused in Jove such ache that "Me, oh! my, oh!"
He cried, "she must be mine!" and when he had the maid deluded
And had some happiness with her, she as a cow concluded.*

*Behind, above, below all modern manners of invention,
Ovid resides, and to the sides, sublime beyond dissension—
Finnegans Wake is wide awake, and Proust so widely ranges;
Stendhal's a wall where roses fall and Blake is full of dangers;
Byron is great, Williams of late, and Shakespeare for the ages;
But what is life, and what is fate, without Ovidian changes?
No place to go, no one to be, stuck in romance's muddle—
There's no escape! There is one, though—you change into a puddle!
Or to a stone that stops lamenting at the puddle's edge
Or to the grass beneath your lady lying on a ledge.
Why be enslaved to human form when there are countless others?
Why be the dull amalgams of our fathers and our mothers?
Is not that eagle soaring there, is not that goldfish bubbling,
Is not that perfume in the air that is so subtly troubling,
Are not all these, are not these bees, so bossy and so buzzing,
A part of us, a gift to us, and close as any cousins?
If I so choose I can amend my speech to make it doglike—
I bark; I grunt to be a pig; I croak and I am froglike;
I raise my arms and spread them out and feel I am a maple;
I touch the floor upon all fours and have become a table.
And when—it happens most in love—I lose my whole identity,
I still am something—clearly, though, I am a different entity.
Without this change what is one but a sort of vegetation
That, once it's planted, grows and shows the rose of expectation,
Then withers and is scissored off and thrown into the barrow?
What if, most fragrant, pinkest, best, one changed into an arrow?
What if, when sitting longing for a life-preserving call,
In tears, you were transformed into a mighty waterfall?
Then could you tolerate the vacant spaces of the night,
Or if you were an olive tree, or shark about to bite.

It happened this way. Jove one morning as he walked along,
Singing a sort of thissy thatsy gay Olympian song,
Beheld a female, Io—and her beauty made him shiver—
Come running from her father's banks (her father was a river,
Inachus, a Thessalian one, who flowed through Tempe Valley—
So many lovely girls have river dads originally!
Rivers who are immortal but must flow against the odds
Being no match, in case of crisis, for the greater gods,
Such as, in this case, Jupiter, who strolling by their waters
May bring great harm because of love intended to their daughters—
And yet, and yet, you'll see when you are finished with this story
They suffer, yes, but often end up consummate with glory—
Io, I'll tell you in advance, was in this category)—
In any case, the King of Gods (as if gods needed rulers—
It's a conception both profound and worthy of pre-schoolers),
The King of Gods espying her, in her bodacious tresses,
Desired for to fuck with her beside the watercresses,
"Where we'll be cool," he said, "and you'll be safe as you are stunning—
I shall protect you—"
                          But she had already started running
And ran through Lerna Marsh and ran through Lincie's budding woods
Till Jove, impatient, brought a fog upon these neighborhoods,
A thick and foggy mist, in which the girl had trouble seeing,
And being lost was to her cost one with Eternal Being—
Which is to say, Jove had his way and pressed himself inside her
And for that portion of the day felt happy as a glider.
      However, Juno, jealous Juno, zealous brunette, looking
At so dark mist on such fair day, demanded what was cooking,
For there was not a river or a marsh or swamp around
That could be sending up such foggy substance from the ground.
Husband! she cried, and went around to all Olympian places
Searching for him but found him not among the bearded faces.

In fact, we are so changed by love that what we recognize
When looking in a mirror is a pitiable disguise.
We are transformed! It is a horror, and it is a glory.
With racing heart and strafing nerves we make the inventory,
But never see it quite so clearly as in Ovid's story—
The clouds, the woods, streams, beasts, and birds, all life's surrounding creatures,
Are what we shall be, were, and are, and bear our loving features.

"Well, I suppose, what else, God knows, he's at his usual capers,
Getting a girl with the assistance of substantial vapors.
We'll put a stop to that!" she said. And, "Mists, be on your way!"
And suddenly above the god it was translucent day.
But Jupiter had seen in time what Juno was about
And by the time she got to earth there was a kind of snout,
Well not snout really but a bovine heightened kind of nose
On Io's face and from her flattened head two horns arose;
Her arms had turned to legs—so she was well-equipped to walk
Close to the ground—her mouth could graze, and gape, but could not talk.
She still was white and pretty though she was a heifer now.
Juno admired her grudgingly. "Where did you find this cow?"
She questioned. "From what herd is she?" And Jupiter replied,
"She sprouted up here from the ground." But Juno knew he lied.
"Darling, she's such a lovely one, I'd like her for a gift."
"Er, well, my dear—"
                              Jove felt some fear. And he had little shrift—
He didn't want to give his sweetheart to his nagging wife,
But also didn't want her nagging at him all his life,
Which was eternal. And it seemed so small a thing to ask—
A cow!—"Of course, all right," he said, his face a pleasant mask,
Although inside he didn't like at all what he was doing.
      The goddess, having got the former Girl, who now was mooing,
Needed to figure out a way to keep her precious prize
Away from Jupiter. And then she thought of Argus' eyes!
One hundred eyes adorned the head of Argus. When he slept
He closed but two (I do not know what happened when he wept)—
In any case, for guardian of a woman or a cow,
No one could watch as Argus could, and his is Io now.
"Let her go out by day," said Juno, "let her roam around,
But when the night comes, fasten her with willows to the ground."
Argus agreed, whose sight was such that Io he discerned
When facing her or to the side or when his back was turned.
She fed on leaves and bitter plants and muddy water drank
And oft at night to rocky ground in restless sleep she sank.
She wanted to stretch out her arms to him in supplication
But had no arms to stretch, and in no way by conversation
Could she excite his pity, but could only moo, and seem
The more a cow.

One day she walked beside her father's stream.
The sun was bright, the air was still, there scarcely was a zephyr—
It made the heart expand even though the heart was in a heifer.
Then, bending down her head, she looked and saw her face reflected:
What gaping jaws, what horrid horns were to her self connected!
She started back in awful fear and bolted here and there;
Her sister naiads petted her to soothe her, unaware
Of course that she was Io. (How she wanted to be one
Of the Inachus girls again, handmaidens of the sun
And wood and way and water, but those days, it seemed, were done!)
Now she was with her sisters, but she walked on hoofy feet;
Was with her father, but was dumb. He brought her grass to eat.
He, miserable, aflood with grief, had searched with no success
For Io everywhere, and did not know and could not guess
Whether she was among the Shades or if she still drew breath—
Since she was nowhere, he feared for her something worse than death.
Distracted now he feeds the pretty cow, who licks his hand.
Weeping, she longs to find some way to make him understand,
And with her hoof she traces her name IO in the sand.
(How fortunate that she was not named Thesmophoriazusa
Or Melancholy Myrtle, or Somatacalapoosa—
For by the time she wrote it out her strength would have been wasted,
Inachus have gone elsewhere, or the rising tide erased it.)
At once her father understood. "Oh woe is me!" he cried
"You are a cow, who were my dear, my darling, and my pride!
I hoped that you would marry soon as other maidens do
And I would have a son-in-law, and have grandchildren, too,
But now I see that it must be a bull who marries you!"
He wept. She wept. He held her close, her horns and all, and said,
"What pain it is to know your pain! I wish that I were dead!
No help to you is to be had, and all to me is futile—
Alas the Gate of Death is closed and I am an immortal!"
Now as her father made lament, Argus with eyes like stars
Removed her from those latitudes and past the Eastern bars
To where she grazed in other pastures; and he found a seat
Atop a mountain where his view of Io was complete.

    Jupiter now had had enough. He didn't want the heifer
Because of Juno's jealousy so horribly to suffer.
He summoned Mercury and said "O nephew of the Pleiade,
Great messenger, enchanter, go, and rescue me my Naiad!"

Whereat the god took up his magic cap and wingèd shoes
And sleep-producing wand—he didn't travel without those—
And came to earth. Pretending he's a goatherd, he advances
Where Argus is, upon a syrinx playing songs and dances.
Argus was smitten by that music. "Come and sit with me.
There's grass for goats and shade for us," he said to Mercury.
    The god agreed, and sat and played sweet notes till Argus dozed
But also stayed awake, since only half his eyes were closed—
Some of those open still kept watch, and others paid attention
To the strange reed-pipe Mercury played, which was a new invention.
When Argus asked about it, Mercury left off playing lyrics
And told him how the pipe was born: of Pan's pursuit of Syrinx,
A wood nymph, fair and much pursued, whose wish it was to be
Diana-like, a huntress, and of perfect chastity—
And when she was attired like her, and when she held her bow,
Whether or not she was Diana it was hard to know.
Many mistook her for the goddess. When she walked one morning
On the cool slopes, and in such guise, the god Pan saw her coming
And felt for her, divinely fair, his godly spirits soaring
And went to her and said to her, "O Maiden, thou art—" Snoring!
Not Syrinx, no, but Argus, of whom the star-studded cranium
Was veiled by eyelids like the undersides of a geranium.
Could this be true? It was. So the remainder of the tale
Argus was destined not to hear—how Pan pursued the pale
And trembling hamadryad till she came to Ladon's banks
And begged to be transformed—she was, to reeds; she murmured, Thanks
Just at the moment racing Pan caught up to her and found
He held no nymph but what best grows on moist and sandy ground,
A bunch of hollow reeds. He sighed. To lose his girl was odious
But what those reeds made of his sigh was haunting and melodious.
Touched by the wonder of the reeds, enchanted by their tone,
Pan said, "In playing, thus, on thee, my dear, we shall be one."
The instrument of reeds forthwith retained the name of Syrinx.
Mercury meanwhile separated Argus at the larynx,
Swiping him with his curving sword, once he had made it certain,
Using his wand, each eyeball slept behind its lidded curtain.
Bounding and bouncing down the rocks, the head of Argus flies,
One single darkness in what used to be a hundred eyes.
Juno, at seeing Argus wasted and herself upstaged,
Was—how could Jove not know she would be?—totally enraged.

First, she took Argus' eyes and placed them in the peacock's tail
Where they would always shine. Then, something sharper than a nail
She set in Io's hide, a terror-causing wasp-like goad
To torture her like fury as she ran down every road
She came to, mad with pain, forgetful even of her shape,
Wishing above all other things that stinging to escape—
Poor Io, tortured out of Greece, to race through alien dust,
Her only crime for a short time to have aroused the lust
Of one who saw her not, as she ran, stumbling in her pain,
On four short legs, until she came upon the waving grain
Of the Nile Delta, then the Nile, that cuts the land in two,
And there she stopped, Great Nile, for having got as far as You,
She could no more. Upon your shore, she lifted up her face
To stars where she thought Jove might be, commanding from that place,
And by her moos and mournful moans, on bent and knobby knees,
From suffering unendurable did beg forthwith surcease.
Jove heard her then. And pleaded, with his arm about his wife,
That she permit him to give Io back her former life.
"Fear not," he said, "she'll be a source of grief to you no more."
"Swear!" Juno said. And by the deadly Stygian pools he swore.
     Juno relents. And Io starts to be herself again,
Her former self that brought delight to gods as well as men.
Her mouth and eyes decrease in size, her gaping jaw deducted,
Rough hair and hide are altered, and her horns are deconstructed.
Ten fingernails appear where were two hooves, and she has hands
And shoulders, and a waist, and, now, upon two legs she stands—
She who had altered from a naiad to a bestial form
Becomes a queenly girl again, too royal for the farm,
And is completely Io (of the cow she keeps the white
And nothing more), but, standing so, she feels a sort of fright,
A fear of speaking—what if she should moo?—but has no choice
And speaks—in words! and owns once more her interrupted voice.

Now she is worshipped as a goddess, with the greatest honor,
After she gives birth to a son perhaps begot upon her
That summer day when, graceful, gay, she ran up from the river
Her father was, and stirred the lust of Jove the Thunder-Giver.

A Time Zone

On y loue des chambres en latin Cubicula locanda.
Je m'en souviens j'y ai passé trois jours et autant à Gouda
APOLLINAIRE, *Zone*

A light from the ceiling is swinging outside on Forty-second Street traffic
    is zinging
Collaborating on The Construction of Boston is interesting
To construct the city of Boston Tinguely is putting up a big wall
Of gray sandstone bricks he is dressed in a French ball
Gown he puts the wall up during the performance
His costume is due to art and not to mental disturbance
Now the wall ten feet high is starting to tremble
People seated in the first rows run back for shelter
However the bricks stand firm Niki de St. Phalle dressed as Napoleon
Shoots at a Venus full of paint with a miniature (but real) cannon
Rauschenberg's rain machine's stuck it gives too much moisture
People look very happy to have gotten out of the theater
People ask that it be put on again but it can't be done
Tinguely with his hand bleeding says Boston can be constructed only once
And that is the end of that
Next day the Maidman Theatre stage is flat
I like the random absurdity of this performance
Done only once with nineteen-sixty-two-and-art romance
I meet Niki four years earlier in France in the spring
Five years before that I am with Janice and Katherine
In Greece two thousand years ago everything came crashing
We stand and try to imagine it from what is still standing
Years before this in Paris it's the boulevard Montparnasse
Larry Rivers is here he is living with a family that includes a dwarf
We are talking I have a "Fulbright" with us is Nell Blaine
I am pulled in one direction by Sweden in another by Spain
The idea of staying in Europe jolts me gives a convincing jerk
It's New York though where most of my friends are and the "new work"
Today with Frank O'Hara a lunch connection
The Museum of Modern Art is showing its Arp collection

Frank comes out of the doorway in his necktie and his coat
It is a day on which it would be good to vote
Autumn a crisp Republicanism is in the air tie and coat
Soon to be trounced by the Democrats personified as a slung-over-the-
   shoulder coat
Fascism in the form of a bank
Gives way to a shining restaurant that opens its doors with a clank
However before being taken into this odoriferous coffer
A little hard-as-a-hat poem to the day we offer
"Sky/woof woof!/harp"
This is repeated ten times
Each word is one line so the whole poem is thirty lines
It's a poem composed in a moment
On the sidewalk about fifteen blocks from the Alice in Wonderland
   Monument
Sky woof woof! harp is published in Semicolon
Later than this in this John Myers publication
O'Hara meanwhile is bending above his shirt
His mind being and putting mine on being on International Alert
There's no self-praise in his gossip
Which in fact isn't gossip but like an artistic air-trip
To all the greatest monuments of America and Europe
Relayed in a mild excited wide open-eyed smiling conversational style
Larry he says and Larry again after a while
He is crazy about Larry these two have a relationship
That is breaking the world's record for loquaciousness
I first meet Larry on Third Avenue
The El goes past and it throws into my apartment rust dust soot and
   what-have-you
Larry has a way of putting himself all out in front of himself
And stumbling through it and looking good while seemingly making fun
   of himself
This is my friend Larry Rivers says Jane Freilicher
She lives upstairs Larry is a sometime visitor
He is dedicated at this moment entirely to drawing
Abstract split-splot and flops and spots he finds a blur and boring
Give me a glass of pencil that hath been
Steeped a long time in Delacroix and Ingres nor does he neglect Rubens
He is drawing up a storm in his studio working hard
A little bit earlier he and Jane and others are bouleversés by Bonnard

Bonnard show at the Modern Museum
I meet these people too late to go and see them
I am of New York not a native
I'm from Cincinnati which is to this place's nominative like a remote dative
In 1948 from college I come here and finally settle
The city is hot and bright and noisy like a giant boiling kettle
My first connection to it aside from touristy is sexual
A girl met here or there at first nothing serious or contextual
That is earlier now I'm here to live on street subway and bus
I find people exciting unrecognizable and of unknown-to-me social class
Finally they start to come into focus
For a while it's like being at a play I may have the wrong tickets
On West Tenth Street now I am firmly settled in New York
I am a poet je suis poète but I'm not doing very much work
I'm in love with a beautiful girl named Robin
Her father has a hand-weaving factory he gives me a job winding bobbins
It is a one-floor loft in the garment district on Thirty-first Street
Pat Hoey visits someone next door on snow-white feet
Pat and I like to go to the ballet at the City Center
I get "Balanchined" as in a wine-press all Jacques d'Amboise has to do is enter
My poetry is somewhat stuck
It's taking me a little while to be able to write in New York
My painter friends help and what I am reading in the library
It is not the contemporary antics this happens later of John Ashbery
This shy and skinny poet comes down to visit me from "school"
When he and Jane Freilicher meet it's as if they'd both been thrown into a
    swimming pool
Afloat with ironies jokes sensitivities perceptions and sweet swift
    sophistications
Like the orchids of Xochimilco a tourist attraction for the nations
Jane is filled with excitement and one hundred percent ironic
This conversation is joy is speed is infinite gin and tonic
It is modernism in the lyrical laconic
Our relationship's platonic
With what intelligence linked to what beauty linked to what grassy gusty
    lurch across the canvas
Jane and her paintings I realize once again happiness
Huh? is possibly going to be available after long absence
Here today in a gray raincoat she appears
The style is laughter the subject may be a cause for tears

Larry has some of the qualities of a stand-up comic
He says of John Myers John Myers he always calls him that
John Myers never John John Myers says he isn't fat
Well doesn't have a fat EAR but look at his stomach
And oft at a party back his head he throws
And plays the piano singing a song he made up "My Nose"
His nose bothers and is thus conquered by Larry Rivers
He's doing a Bonnardesque painting it's so good it gives me "recognition"
    shivers
It's a room filled with women with somewhat beautiful fishlike graces
Mostly orangey-yellow they have sexy and sleepy looks on their faces the
    thick
Oil paint makes it look as if you'd stick
To it if you got next to it it also looks very spacious
Now Larry is sitting and smiling he is copying an Ingres
His hand is shaky his lines are as straight as coat hangers
Why don't you I say rather dumbly put something witty in your work
No Kenneth I can't he says prancing around like a funny Turk
Charcoal in one hand and making a little gesture with the other
One Sunday I go with him to the Bronx to visit his sister and his mother
Here I am with Larry's sister and his mother
Sitting in the kitchen above us is a motto
Joannie is blonde her brunette friend is warm and flushed as a risotto
I rather fancy her and Larry's mother fancies it stupid
To have invited this girl at the same time as me so interrupting the arrow of
    Cupid
Posing for Rivers his mother-in-law Berdie before a screen
Posing for her son-in-law this woman full and generous as the double issue of
    a magazine
The French *Vogue* for example or the *Ladies Home Journal*
Frank thinks her marvelous he finds the sublime in her diurnal
Larry is making a leafy tree out of metal
Here is his Jewish version of Courbet's painting of a funeral
Jane loves Matisse and is a fan of Baudelaire
In these paintings she is working on a secret of yellow blue and pink air
She and Larry make a big painting together
Larry with an unmeditated slash Jane with the perpetuity of a feather
That in a breeze is trying to pull itself together
I'm looking at the finished product it's rather de Kooningesque

Being de-Kooning-like some way is practically of being a New York painter
    the test
Here today though is not a de Kooning but one of Jane's it's luscious big and
    feminine
I am inspired by these painters
They make me want to paint myself on an amateur basis
Without losing my poetic status
Jane is demonstrating to me the pleasures of using charcoal
I am copying a Delacroix of a black woman called I think The Slave Girl
Erasing makes a lovely mess
It looks like depth and looks like distance
Ink at the opposite end of materials is deliberate and daring
No chance to erase it and oil pastels like wildflowers in a clearing
My Aesthetic I only paint for a few years is rather elementary
Get something that looks good looks real looks surprising looks from this
    century
I am sitting at a little table downstairs in the Third Avenue apartment
I like buying slabs of masonite and all kinds of equipment
At the Metropolitan on a big wall is a great big Rubens
Of a king and some nobles on horses bigger than cabins
I am walking through the European Collection
With Larry and Jane they're giving it a professional inspection
On drawing paper I'm doing some Seurat-like dotting
I like this even love it but I know it's going to come to nothing
It is invigorating to stand in this studio
John Ashbery comes to visit he is listening to Bob and Ray on our radio
It is a small old-fashioned console attacked by salt water
John finds them wheezingly amusing all over the house sounds his raucous
    laughter
He and I "go back" to Harvard College
Now he is sitting at his typewriter in Greenwich Village
He's just finished a poem and he's happy as after a good repast
He is certain this feeling won't last
John is predictably and pleasantly gloom-filled
I've just driven to New York from some place north of Bloomfield
I'm an hour and a half late
This enables John to finish his poem as I with mixed feelings find out
"The Picture of Little J.A. in a Prospect of Flowers"
He made good use of this couple of wasted hours

Dick gives Genevieve a swift punch in the pajamas
It's a vault over W. C. Williams and a bypass of Dylan Thomas
He is still sitting at his little portable
Being because of my poem-causing lateness exceptionally cordial
We are both fans of the old Mystery Plays
We also find each other mysterious in certain ways
This mystery becomes greater as more time passes
Then finally the mystery itself passes
We're at Harvard together
We walk along talking about poetry in the autumn weather
He is not writing much this year but he likes to collaborate
So do I we do a set of sestinas at a speedy rate
Six sestinas each about an animal with one concluding one called The
    Bestiary
There is also a three-page poem in which all the lines rhyme with the title
    The Cassowary
Next we do a poetic compendium called The New York Times
September Eighth Nineteen Fifty-One both with and without rhymes
Our poems are like tracks setting out
We have little idea where we're going or what it's about
I enjoy these compositional duets
Accompanied by drinking coffee and joking on Charles and Perry Streets
We tell each other names of writers in great secret
Secret but absolutely no one else cares so why keep it
We're writing a deliberately bad work called The Reconstruction of
    Colonial Williamsburg
In a feeble attempt to win a contest the style is the Kenyon Review absurd
Larry and Jane propose to me renting a house in East Hampton
We go sizzling out of the city with the rapidity of a flu symptom
No this is actually a year later my memory missed it
I now go to California to be a "teaching assistant"
This year goes by I meet the girl who is later my wife Janice
I love to kiss her and to talk to her very often it's talking about my friends
I also talk a lot about "Europe" and France
She's a little deflating and tells me that to be a great poet
I have to do something she tells me but I forget exactly what
I think have for all my poems some sort of system
I am shaken but still feel secure in my avant-garde wisdom
East Hampton glaringest of Hamptons Hampton of sea shine of de Kooning
    and of leaves

Frank's visiting we're composing a poem he tugs at his sleeves
It is a Nina we are composing it is a Nina Sestina
For Nina Castelli's birthday her adorable sixteenth one
This year this month this week in fact Frank writes "Hatred"
A stunning tour-de-poem on an unending roll of paper
It makes going on forever seem attractive
Writing in the manner of O'Hara means being extremely active
Twenty people are over then thirty now about forty
Zip Frank sits down in the midst and types out a poem it doesn't even seem
    arty
I try it out with little success
It's one of those things the originator can do best
"Hatred" is full of a thundering array of vocables
From it straight through to the Odes Frank's talent is implacable
Now here he is holding out to me a package
Of Picayunes he taps one on his kneebone-covering khakis
Finally we have a poem for Castelli's daughter
Moonlight dissolve next day we're visiting Anne and Fairfield Porter
Fairfield is in his studio a mighty man
Posing like fluttering then settling sea birds around him Jerry Katie
    Elizabeth and Anne
He has opinions that do not waver
On his canvases he creates a bright and wholesome fever
Flowers like little pockets of yellow and pink pigment
Are aspiring up to a tree or a wall or a house like a sunlight shipment
At a John Cage concert there is hardly a sound
It's the paradise of music lost and music found
I find it pure and great as if a great big flash of light were going off
    underground
Satie and Webern are hitting me in the head and so finally with the Cantos
    is Ezra Pound
Frank and I are writing very long poems
Long is really the operative word for these poems
His is called Second Avenue mine When the Sun Tries to Go On
I don't know where I got the title
I'm working on it every afternoon the words seem to me arriving like
    stampeding cattle
It's not at all clear but for the first time in my life the words seem
    completely accurate
If I write for three hours I allow myself a cigarette

I'm smoking it's a little too much I'm not sure I can get through it alone
Frank and I read each other segments of these long works daily on the
    phone
Janice finds it funny now that I've dropped this bunch of pages
That I can't get them back in the right order well I do but it's by stages
It is April I have a job at the Hunter College Library
I come down to the Cedar on a bus hoping to see O'Hara and Ashbery
Astonishingly on the bus I don't know why it's the only occasion
I write a poem Where Am I Kenneth? It's on some torn-out notebook pages
The Cedar and the Five Spot each is a usable place
A celebrated comment Interviewer What do you think of space? De Kooning
    Fuck space!
In any case Frank is there he says he likes Where Am I Kenneth?
I carry this news home pleasantly and the poem it mentions her to Janice
John's poem Europe is full of avant-garde ardor
I am thinking it's making an order out of a great disorder
I wonder at what stage in life does this get harder
The Cedar Bar one hardly thinks of it is what may be called a scene
However one closed to the public since no one goes there to be seen
It is a meeting place for the briefest romances
And here is Norman Bluhm at the bar saying Who cares about those nances?
And here he is shoving and here is de Kooning and there is a beer
Being flung at someone Arnold Weinstein or me through the smoke-talky
    atmosphere
Of this corner booth
Voici Guston and Mitchell and Smith and here on top of everything is Ruth
Kligman being bedazzling without stop
She writes a poem with the line At the bar you've got to be on top
Meanwhile tonight Boris Pasternak
Is awarded the Nobel Prize and is forced to give it back
Frank O'Hara is angry there seems both a flash and a blur in his eyes
Kenneth we've got to do something about Pasternak and the Nobel Prize
What? well we ought to let him know
That we support him Off flies a cable into the perpetual snow
Dear Boris Pasternak We completely support you and we also love your
    early work
Signed puzzlingly for him in the morning's glare if he ever receives it
    Frank O'Hara and Kenneth Koch
Staging George Washington Crossing the Delaware
Alex Katz comes up looking like a pear

He has some white plywood boards with him he says where
Shall I put this stuff and a big bare
Wall is the side of their emplacement No chair
For Alex painting and cutting And now they're there
The seven soldiers one cherry tree one Delaware crossing boat
Hey hey Ken cries Alex I've done it
I've made you a set for George Washington Crossing the Delaware
The British and American armies face each other on wooden feet
I write this play in our apartment on Commerce Street
I am working in the early afternoon and stay up late
Dawn is peeling oranges on top of the skyscrapers
On the stage a wall goes up and then it's taken down
And under the Mirabeau Bridge flows the Seine
Today Larry and Frank are putting together "Stones"
It's a series of lithographs
Larry puts down blotches violently they look like the grapes of wrath
Frank is smoking and looking his best ideas come in transit
I walk the nine blocks to the studio he says Come in
New York today is white dirty and loud like a snow-clogged engine
Huge men in undershirts scream at each other in trucks near Second
       Avenue and Tenth Street
De Kooning's landscapey woman is full of double-exposure perfections
Bob Goodnough is making some small flat red corrections
Jane is concentrating she's frowning she has a look of happy distress
She's painting her own portrait in a long-sleeved dark pink dress
I'm excited I'm writing at my typewriter it doesn't make too much sense

The First Step

A journey of ten thousand li begins with the first step.

In the country of the middle
The person in the middle is king
No one walking on the outskirts
No sprechstimme singing in Beijing

Splash of water at the end of the ship
Flash of sky at the end of the plane
Dash of suit at the end of the man
Clash of music going away

There is no moulding
There is no "souk"
There is no pounding and no landing
Nothing but Chinese absence soup

A journey of five hundred limits
Begins with the first one met
After the first, one knows that this is not
The "real" journey and yet and yet

No Africa, no rest of Asia, no Europe no sweet continent
No Italy no England no Portugal no Spain
And Spain exists outside the scientific revolution
As Sicily exists outside it, no Brazil, no Cuba, only China

One sensuous life and three parks
Two kinds of government eighteen minority nationalities
One woman two women a man three
A long corral of roofs a boat an evening

The new dawn rises
With the first ray of the sun
Why are you going away?
From the born smoke rises

The first whisper of departure starts in his nostrils
It starts there though it comes from far away
His life today is like a stereopticon
He sees more than at any other time

No chamber orchestra to say when you have arrived there
No religious chorus to say when you have gotten there
No French horn section to say when at last you are there
Only a beat de-tuck-tucking of a single heart

Seventeen intellectuals on a train
The train is not going nowhere
Inside it as it is going somewhere
The intellectuals' minds are moving around

Panda on a stamp
Hing Chow post office
Panda on a stage
Beijing Zoo

"Call Amalgamated Chinoiseries and get me the manager!
Give me a bowl of the share-holding poundings of the sea!
Let them be like flowrets on my army bandage!
I want to never leave the hinges of this diamond sleep!"

So much depends upon
The room temperature
Hitches up skirt. He lifts
Phonograph needle. Day fleets down.

The basket of laundry starts on Huang Yin Street
It moves through the crowded city with a bustle of napkins
Finally it arrives at the large hotel
There it is undone like a flapping of wings

I have never
Seen such streets
Such had never
Sight of me

Man woman baby bicycle basket
Truck crossroad vanishing composite northern
Great Wall resolute slow
Table rock needle tire sting

With song of self pity denigrated by taste
Soaring apathetic and night-canoey
Walking along streets that seem going to waste
Outside Paris and in Shanghai and Huan-Shi City

If only you had come
When the need was highest
Romantic hooey
But some drenched train

Green moss scabs the sides of trees
Wisteria-reaches clutch the wood railing of the porch
A diet is proposed: Don't eat.
The point of life is discussed: Sleep together.

The walls of this farmhouse
Are made of stone
Everyone thinks
To live a long time

In the post office
No postage meter
No automatic box to give stamps
No special delivery and no federal express

Showers fall down
He is unhappy
Out comes the sun
Shakes off and smiles

He speaks crop language
To farm analysts
Beside the white
Un-analyzed chickens

Skeletons in Salvadorean pits
Black needles of Hong Kong
Ships burning like coats eagles like aprons
Gas the good air of paradise turned to stench

At the poultry market
The sun shines. A chicken jumps up
At the sea-bait market
A snail jumps up

These pink Chinese characters, San She Dan Chen Pills!
Two birds with blue back-feathers
Lean over a spray of blossoms white and pink
Take them for your health Signature baseball
Followed by the author's explanation

Post office has stamps yellow color green blue orange red brown
Many picture panda embrace follow plus leaders ruling men
Lick of stamp to other side come glue and postal paste fellow
Bringing a lamp to mailbox show by light how get them in

No stopping those officials on the way to the airport
No reasoning with them to about-face
No saying Better to stop and have a good time
Good time for them is this not our good time

He was sorry to be so angry
He was sorry to be so nervous
He was sorry to be so absent
He was sorry to be so stunned

No soft breast
No soft bottom
No soft sleeper
No one on the train

After a mile
No more music
After five miles
No more news

While she was there
While he is here
Pink buds blossom
In the People's Park

The baby is not a soft sleeper but a hard sleeper
The train from Kunming to Shanghai the baby runs on alone

How amazing to see so many hundreds
Of international celebrities at once!
They are all in a picture on a poster
They stand pasted to a billboard—lucky ones

The automobile holds still
Inside is Official
The automobile moves
The Official sits back and smiles

Only canal with muddy boat
Purple what-have-you
First mate smiling
Second or third face smiling

Perimeter of lake
People very busy
Only one loony-seeming man
Stands and screams before Authorities

Moment to hush those talkies
Very strange man
Feminine police mood filling cabinet
Very very strange man

In head no thought
On heart no scar
In mouth no word
Dead so far

The Shanghai skyscrapers shine like fire of dragons
The Huangpu River Bridge is like a palace woman's hairpin
The People's Park is like a jungle without trees or animals
The people crowded on the boat are like boxes in a store

No fish on menu
No meat on menu
No vegetable on menu
No rice no tea

The young day ruins itself for democracy
The blue river stabs itself into trees

No Beijing Opera
No King with red face
No King with white face
No Queen with whitish-blue face

Ivy falling forward
Over gray great wall
Men seeming lacking in compassion
Driving a human pile-driver twenty miles long

She wakes up goes to market
A fine white hen flies to the floor
She tries to pick it up
But she does not have enough yuan

The soft sleeper leaves the city at dawn
The hard sleeper leaves at the same time
One sleeper is attached to the other sleeper
Rolling quietly they are the same train

Today in the dimness
Nine persons eating Dim Sum
Tonight in the darkness
Ninety-seven persons eating shark

No pigs standing in front of the grocery store
No wagon of cow manure stopped in the middle of the major road
No huge advertisements for doctors in the center of the square
No women tugging their husbands through canal pits thick with mud

No burning face from suddenly-fired sexual excitement
No teacher with white hand turning away embarrassed and pleased
No warrior with grim expression keeping watch
No herbalist no pencils no camera salesman nothing four hundred city blocks

No banners signalling reprieve from someone's dying
No reverse funeral body up others beneath
No birth changing baby gives birth to mother
Everything happens reply to question long ago set

In the room she sits and sews
Seventeen seventy seven
In the boat he so painfully rows
Nine hundred and ten

This farm man's forcefulness begins in childhood
It rides through adolescence and into manhood
There gathering into a personal and/or social clump
It dazzling leaps forward and achieves nothing or something

No back of the basement
No Egyptian tile replacement
No oaken stuff
Only an under-ample yuan disbursement

The schoolteacher stands
Waving his hand sideways
The car backs in
That brings the Official to his school

No boat no pyramid in this part of town
No float no cinnamon in this part of town
No coast guard in this part of town
No École des beaux arts in this part of town

No fat women
No fat crowds
No fat safety police
No fat fowls

Engine
Sea gull
Fold up
Flash

Amoeba serena
Cows ilk
Uncomprehending
Sample of speech: "Whiff"

What do you write about? "Four Modernizations
Modernization of agriculture, of education,
Of industry, of science" The poets' explanation
"We write about the Four Modernizations"

Eternally weather of spring
Sixty-seven degrees temperature sing

No room on airplane Shanghai Kunming
No room on airplane Queylin Hanshu
No soft sleeper
Only hard sleeper journey five days

Suddenly wakes up man room
Bed rumpled dirty several newspaper
Table cup little dishes tea leaves
Meiyou What do you want

Dancers on stage in the theatre
Cow at the end of a rope
In the field
Gray dog sitting by a wall

Nothing moving in lifeboat
No one walking in corridor
Only in main salon lobby
Magician describe take handkerchief

Suddenly losing interest
Suddenly losing narrow
Suddenly losing valley
Suddenly losing train

No snow on the gate to the Forbidden City
No snow on the Hall of Felicitous Harmony
No snow on the Pathway of Endless Peace
No sun there either

Empty empty
Quiet quiet
Thousand thousand
Sleep and stand

The panda in the Beijing Zoo
Is a minority nationality
The panda in the American zoo
Is overseas Chinese

In and out in and out of traffic goes the car
Drops of rain fall on the Huangpu River
Someone bends forward with anxiety
Another bends back with the machine

When the car comes back
The back seat is empty
When the car sets out
Its seat contains one

Bed is absent
Breast is absent
Bend is absent
Bet is absent

No Western prescriptions
No Vicks VapoRub and no Anacin
No Empirin no Kotex no Trojan rubbers
Only jars of deer horn ground to powder

"Into my brain pattern noxious Occident
Stoop is restful in rain battering uncopying Orient
A glad dry, a roomy husk, pretensions
But later a soothing cry, abrasions, summing up."

Light on water
What is this?
Little boat with light
What light is this?

A man on the boat
A line in the water
A line around the park
Of bushes and trees

Poems by Ships at Sea

*It was not known that ships at sea wrote poetry. Now it
is known. Captain Henry Dreyfus has recorded some of
these Pacific and Atlantic songs, most of them composed
by large, cargo-bearing vessels of the Dutch, British,
Portuguese and French lines. One poem, the last, is by
an American ship.*

BEARING CARGO

By the SS Van Djik of the Dutch and Homburg Line

Bearing cargo, heavy cargo over the plain
Level friction of the water, I sometimes see
A delicate ship waving to me from the distance
And I go more swiftly, as if to carry my weight to her knees.
Alas, she vanishes
Before I become acquainted with the night
Of the first day out—
But, on the second, she is there again!

Atlantic Ocean, near Cape Verde, September 1919

AUTUMN LEAVES

By the HMS Mother of God of the British Catholic or "Lesser" Navy

In autumn the leaves fall
From the maples the oaks the birches
But not on me
For I go far from them
As if I were unburdened,
Suddenly, of all that is heavy in existence,
All that is tainted and painted
All that is dead and all that bears (even fading) life.
Such is my journey—without seasons I sail toward you,
Final Harbour, who are the mother of life.

Location unknown, 1920s

BOXERS

By the SS Oporto, Portuguese Line

Boxers sometimes try to stabilize
The energy of their feet and their haunches
Standing on my waving decks exchanging punches
One topples. Knockout! Yet
He wasn't so hard hit. No it was I
Making a swerve or knocking back a wave
Unwitting. He gets up and tries to pit
His strength against a human force and mine.
I'll try, but can't do much, to let him win.

South Atlantic, off the coast near Swakopmuna (Walvis Bay), 1949

BRAGAN

By the RFSS Messieurs-Dames, French Merchant Export Lines

Way over the expanding water
There is an island, called "Bragan"
Which means "alone one" in Javanese.
This island is alone in the middle of the sea
As a woman may be alone
In the middle of a crowd or when she is with no one
And as a man may be
Anywhere, in a mass of persons, alone,
Or with others, when he is not with this woman,
And as I, the *Messieurs-Dames*, am alone—
And as she will be home to me,
This island, this woman, this Bragan.

Indian Ocean, 11/24/1926

AMERICAN FOAM

By the USS United States, United States Navy

You can talk about the Banda's crazy waters
Where mermaids splash around and kiss and comb
You can yak about the Andaman and Flores
But there's nothing like American foam.

You can say I wish that I were in the Tasman
Or that the Laptev froze me to a stone
But I will tell you, lads, that there is nothing
As soothing and as cooling as the foam

That slaps my keel when I am in Penobscot
Or Tampa Bay, or, when I'm heading home,
The West Atlantic and the East Pacific
Or Puget Sound, or Norton, close to Nome.

There's nothing like the feel of U.S. water
It's straight and sharp and clear and it alone
Can make a ship feel she is Ocean's daughter
Carried upon her parent's shoulders home.

(probably) Tasman Sea, 1930s

Talking to Patrizia

Patrizia doesn't want to
Talk about love she
Says she just
Wants to make
Love but she talks
About it almost endlessly to me.

It is horrible it
Is the worst thing in life
Says Patrizia
Nothing
Not death not sickness
Is as bad as love

I am always
In love I am always
Suffering from love
Says Patrizia. Now
I am used to it
But I am suffering all the same

Do you know what I did to her
Once?—speaking
Of her girlfriend—I kicked her out
I literally kicked her she was down on the floor and I
Gave her the colpi di piedi the
Kicks of my foot. She slided out.

She did this
To me promised to go on a trip
I am all waiting prepared
Suitcases and tickets
She comes and says her other friend finds out she
Can't go she guessed about it. I KICKED her out

Oh we are still together
Sometimes. But love is horrible. I thought
You might be the best
Person to talk to Patrizia since you
Love women and are a woman
Yourself. You may be right Patrizia

Said. But this woman who abandons
You I think you should
Disappear. Though maybe with this woman
Disappearing won't work.
I think not disappear.
It's too bad I don't know her

If I knew her if I could see her
Just for ten minutes—I'm afraid
If you saw her you might take
Her away from me. Patrizia
Laughs. No it hasn't happened to me
Thank God to like such young women yet

Why? When you are my
Age—still young—she
Is thirty . . . nine? you are close enough
To people very young to
Know how horrible they are
And you don't love them

You don't want to have anything
To do with them! Oh
Uh huh, I said putting
My hands down on the table and then off
Look at you excuse me but I have to laugh
At you sitting in this horrible

Restaurant at one o'clock
In the morning in a
City you don't want to be
In and why? For this woman.
It is horrible I know but
Also funny

I know I said. Listen I have
An idea. Do you know her address? You know where
She lives? You should go there
Go and hide there
Outside her house
In the bushes

Then when she comes out
You jump out
You confront her. You will see
If there is love
In her eyes or not. It can't
Be hidden. You will know It can't be mistaken

This works This has always worked
For me. It won't work for me. I can't
Go and hide there It is true
Patrizia says when there is love everything
Works when there isn't nothing does. Love
Is a god These Freudian things I don't believe at all

This god you have to do what
He wants you to you are
Angry but all you really want
Is to get her back. Then—revenge! If
This woman did something like this to me
I would simply dislike her in fact

I would hate her You may want to consider
Patrizia said that this woman is
Doing this test to you. No, I
Said. I know she's not. I know something. I feel
A hundred years old. Yet
You don't look so bad, Patrizia said.

Find another woman. I can't. I
Know Patrizia said. But one always thinks it
Is a good idea. But
If you can't you can't. I
Can't even eat
This food Patrizia I said.

I'm sorry I said Patrizia to be so
Boring I can't stop talking Forgive
Me. It doesn't bore me at all
Patrizia says It's my favorite subject
It isn't every day one sees somebody
In such a state you can help him by talking to stay alive

You know, Patrizia says if she
Does this thing to you now
She will do it again
And again so you'd better be ready
Maybe you can get the advantage
By saying she is right you

Don't love her Good bye You leave
However if you want her
You should go into the bushes
And surprise her when they see you
It always makes a difference
I can't go hide there Patrizia

That's insane. I went but not
Hiding and not confronting.
Patrizia: What did she say? I said
The same things. Patrizia said
Did you see love in her eyes? I said
No. I didn't. I saw

Something else. In Florence it's rainy
Her (relatively) short hair and
Her eyes along the Arno
The last time I'll ever see her again
As the one I am seeing again
When seeing again still has some meaning.

It's finished Patrizia's saying
For now but don't worry
I think you will get her back
But it will be too late. Oh Patrizia I
Let my back and head fall against
The chair Late isn't anything!

At the Opera

Ah do you remember
                    the voice of Gianni Poggi
                                        in Firenze
"in tuo splendor'"
                    the clear light
                                    and easy division
of the Italian language
                        "aurora" so it sounds like
                                                Bobby Burns
it's another sign
                    Katherine is two—
                                    not quite—grand opera
and you still alive
                    "lucevan le stelle"
                                    and Gozzanno
in the morning
                    the true pink light
                                    and Gatto, the cat
who walked to our doorstep
                                from higher
                                        on the hill
I think, that led
                    someplace (Fiesole?)—
                                        "led" che splendore, "led"
and we, we were
                    led
                        Gianni Poggi was led
He was leading
                    but not the orchestra
                                        led
to his death
                alla sua morte
                                che orror'
but not
        a real one
                    he
was still alive
                when we left
                            the theatre and came home.

No One Else

I could never have had anything
Quite as radical as all this
Was by reason of having known it
Was very soon to go away
As that movie went away from the little theatre
Crossed by our liberal eyes

The other glass by the beam
Orphaning the house with its bulbs
Its way-walks like tusks
And the cut-up scenes
That straightened the glasses
The steam that shows is knowing everything
Is the fax to a fax of itself

At daytime water came unsyphoned
Spoofing our house
I wore a net necktie a button
Or trees with a breeze for a mouth
But nothing could prevent it
As nothing north or south

A bagpipe failed you like Elijah
Women came forth
Reading and tacking fishnets to a port
An old woman rode in a hansom
Beer was an invidious sport

Idiot agreement—and summer tide
These seemed like works to be taught
One kept walking
"Yours to tour but mine to seek from birth"
Cadillacs wrecked
Forgotten and evenings
Boat-flat similar and signed: "No one else."

L'art d'être grand-père

We like the reticent muscle of these days
Enduring what we have to in order to kiss a lot;
Now the art of being a grandfather sits up on my days
With the look of someone hot
"I'll grab you where the matter's at with praise,"
It says, "and take whatever grade you've got
To give to yourself for what you've done to days
During and up till now your lifetime spot."
I said I didn't deserve another's praise;
Saying I thought my achievements might be rot.
"Maybe," my art said, starting to peel off stays,
"But who you are is like to what is what
And when you've risen as you best can raise
Yourself, the day is here and you are not, but that is not"—
And here it stopped, my art—"the end of praise."
"Which, rather?" I demanded, and was shot,
Shot by I know not what, but other days
Must fall as they are falling and are not.
The lifetime of each person is a phase
That paves the ways but never saves the lot—
That is for others' days and waves to spot.

To be alive at all is to amaze
Someone who, looking around, might see a lot
But not a single person; then he prays
That you won't hurt him. You say, "Of course not,"
For you are full of civilizing ways
And don't destroy even when your temper's hot
Though sometimes younger years caught in a maze
Would do their goddamned damnedest to get out
And hit out in all ways
But now concede what pays
The child is on the way—what's that about
It isn't like the mention in a phrase
Of Christ or Colin Clout
It's more like rays

You have to hear this shout
Bareness is coming out
Into a very corridor of praise
Switching about
Until we can adorn it with bouquets
Because of all the ways of turning out
Pleasure to meet the measure of our days
A year, I thought, could be made up of Mays
But what of Guinevere and Lancelot?
They are in a time syndrome like the clays
Infinite Sculpture throws into the pot
And must go later, as I kiss these days
I kiss, they go, they leave us like a shot
Not even clear to us what they're about
Except that what they are about they're not
But something else which, gone a little ways
May turn around and tell us we have got
Something but they can't help us. Oh the ways
We ran each which way trying to work it out
And run each which way trying to work it out,
For grandfather's is not the end of days—
Whoever's sitting in this burning spot
Deserves to figure out
The matchstick and the kindling of these days
When forward steam is not. But still is not.

A reminiscent peacock bunch of plays
I wrote when I was feeling pretty hot
Could persuade nobody to mend his ways
Or become a heroic astronaut
They bent the status quo into a maze
And sent the verse lines jabbering like jays
Across the fragments, kissing in a daze
And I was sad and happy with my lot
I struck at foul confusion with a mace
Of interlocking ways of looking out
Making the wind my messenger of face
But now great sorrow for those aching years, they're gone like mace
Swift evanescence for a mugger's face
And mired in mud is every Camelot

I ever did imagine, not a trace
Is there as I pull in the vacant lot
By vacant lot of thee, old Samothrace,
And think about the art d'être grand-père.
How musically there
A trumpet sounds or slot machine or car
And dims my lifeboat with ten waves of care,
But never separate, knowing you are there,
Which to the best intents of time we are, you are.

Hurrah in praise
Of what is said will still be staying there
The sculptures of infinity's last days
Which cannot be imagined and cannot
Exist in any but imagined ways
And so is our existence on this spot
What splendid days
Anointed, glassed out, pinned, expressive days,
Impressive days, days which to figure out
Which bring the baby like a tiger out
Of his befriending den to give a shout
To mend the cataclysmic trend of days
So human fears know what they are about:
Never to know again the painter's art
And never more the Chevrolet shall start
With who inside it, you inside or out—
This is the very palliative of art
To make you a conundrum on the spot
Which you can burn but never make it blaze
A dream comes stammering out
But only is a dream and that is that
The art of being grand-père finds me out
In searching me through catacombs of rays
To make me stay and state what it's about
To have so rugby-like a field of praise.
Matters to matters, time is in its phase
I fold the rug but I the rug am not
To go through distance and the first of days.
Some man comparing princes being shot
Came up with an unmemorable phrase

Which every king's original forgot
But I'll remember it one of these days
When baby has decreed it shall come out
Making the spinning earth its messenger
Of all that it's about.

On Aesthetics

AESTHETICS OF TAKING A WALK

You
Put
One
Foot
In
Front
Of
The
Other.

AESTHETICS OF THE LITTLE HOUSE

The little house in Italy
Looks good in ports.

AESTHETICS OF BEING A BIRD

Eat brusquely
With a half-closed mouth;
When another speaks, glance up
But don't respond.
After you have eaten
Take off
And sing
Portuguese songs—a fado, if you please!

AESTHETICS OF VICTOR HUGO

Place the Poet in the valleys
Place the Poet in the hills
Let the hills and the valleys
Know that the Poet is there.

AESTHETICS OF THE MAN IN THE MOON

To be the man in the moon
You have to be sunny.

AESTHETICS OF CREATING LIGHT

Put one hand
Next to a light-switch
With the other hand
Feeling for the wall.

AESTHETICS OF FAMILY PICNIC

Take a basket
Of food and drink
And two children
(Aged five and three),
With your husband, the painter,
As close as you can get
To the sea.

AESTHETICS OF OBITUARY

To avoid the clichés
Of the obituary writers,
Die in obscurity.
A fine bed in a light-filled room
Someone who adores you is at your side
And vowed to silence.

AESTHETICS OF STANDING UP

Keep one foot
On the floor
At the same time keeping
The other foot firmly at its side.
Then stand.

AESTHETICS OF HARSHNESS TO A HORSE

You should never be harsh
To a horse. A horse is always doing
Its best. Otherwise it is a bad horse
And harshness has no effect.

AESTHETICS OF CLIMBING STAIRS

With a carpet in the middle
With friends,
With the certainty of love

O friends
O certainty of love!

AESTHETICS OF PAUL VALÉRY

Better a single line that I have worked on
Than a whole epic dictated by the Muse!
Better to walk, even lost, in my own direction—and find the way.
If not . . . not count the day.

AESTHETICS OF BEING A SAILBOAT

Go this way and that
Have a reflection
Be upside down

AESTHETICS OF BABY

Seat yourself on the floor
Bend your trunk forward
Head outstretched with hands reaching
And crawl.

AESTHETICS OF AVANT-GARDE THEATRE

Make the stage an actor
Make an actor the stage.

AESTHETICS OF BEING WITH CHILD

You have the kid
Within what hid
That once did serve
Some lesser curve

So shall the wit
Of having it
Be inly lit
By white by light of day.

AESTHETICS OF FRIENDSHIP

A world without friendship
Is a world without forms.

AESTHETICS OF OTHER LANGUAGES

A young woman without a word
Of English to her vocabulary
Sang like a bird
To a Huguenot student in the moss of February.

AESTHETICS OF GENEROSITY

Give love as a gift
But use your brain.

AESTHETICS OF WAKING UP

Close one eye
After the other.
Whisper "Good-bye!"
To the Unconscious.

AESTHETICS OF BEING ELEPHANTS

When the elephants came to town
The dry cleaning establishments came with them.

AESTHETICS OF BEING THE YOUNGEST
OF FOUR SISTERS

Take a day off
While your sisters are working
Work on a day
When your sisters are taking off
Be bright in the kitchen
Be sullen in the pantry
When they listen to music, cough
When they go to their lovers, be sultry
There is no solution
To being the youngest sister
The hottest summer day
To you is the most wintry
Take your shirt off
And read a while.

AESTHETICS OF BEARS

To be a bear, be active
In the bear world—
Fur, limbs, and claws.
Rampage. Stay. Mate.
Give birth to another bear.

AESTHETICS OF PEARLS

Pearls on a necklace
Are not anything
Compared to pearls
In a late fourth-century Greek frieze.

AESTHETICS OF AIR

Serafina said E bello avere
Nell'appartamento un po
Di natura meaning the window
That let in the sky

AESTHETICS OF VERLAINE AND RIMBAUD

De la musique avant toute chose—Happiness
From which no one gets away.

AESTHETICS OF OTHER WOMEN

They are general and ephemeral;
Your quarrels are engraved in stone.

AESTHETICS OF CLOUDS

Sometimes be red
As Lipstick Number Two;
At others pink
As Corinne on the brink
Of loving you, and saying so,
And also sometimes white
As news at night.

AESTHETICS OF GREEK NIGHT

In the Greek night
The statues
Of Athena and of Apollo
Are no longer white
But painted
In many colors
As they used to be
Two thousand years ago.

AESTHETICS OF BEING GEESE

It is always rush hour
When you are honking.

AESTHETICS OF CREATING TIME

To create time
Relinquish space—that is, the place
Where the time used to be.

AESTHETICS OF ECHO

Echo was   Us
A nymph who lived in   Din
Every cliff.   If

AESTHETICS OF CIVILIZATION

Every dog has the whiff of civilization.
A priest plays ball in the street
With some schoolboys. The overworked chambermaid
Smiles like a duchess.
Even a beggar is addressed as Monsieur or Madame.

AESTHETICS OF PLATO

There has to be something better
Than what we see. Otherwise, we'd see it.

AESTHETICS OF BEING A
BASEBALL

Go as fast as you can
In whatever direction.

AESTHETICS OF CÉZANNE

To have painted
the apples
that were in
the orchard
so red
and so gold.

AESTHETICS OF LOVING AN AZTEC

Be careful of your heart
Or the Aztec will rip it out.

AESTHETICS OF SMALL THEATRE

Don't bring a horse
Into a small theatre
But, if you must,
Put it on stage.

AESTHETICS OF SURREALISM

To find the impossible
With breasts.

AESTHETICS OF ROUGH ART

Smash smudge and erase
So that the true lovely face
Will emerge or maybe will not
But at least you've given it a shot
Somehow characteristic of the age.

AESTHETICS OF MULTIPLICITY OF AESTHETICS
(IN BOTTICELLI'S BIRTH OF VENUS)

In The Birth of Venus, these are some
Of the aesthetics to consider: the aesthetics of shape,
Of line, of color, of contrast, of shadow, of sea clouds, of sky,
Of filmy drapery, of cherubs, of angels, of sunlight,
Of waves, of water, of posture, of hair, of hairdo,
Of wind, of breeze, of puffed cheeks, of the marvelous,
Of realism, of mythology, of paganism, of antiquity, of seeing,
Of allegory, of perfection, of the "exact moment," of sea shells,
Of shoulders, of eyes, of gazing, of breasts, of waists, of feet—

For each of these one has an ideal conception
Whether conscious or unconscious, and when one sees
The Birth of Venus one is moved by, and may think about, these things.

AESTHETICS OF FEET

To move together
Even when apart.

AESTHETICS OF AFTER THE OPERA

When the singing has stopped
The silence of the singing begins
If you are the opera.

AESTHETICS OF DANTE

Invite your best friends
To go out with you in a boat
That's magic and can go anywhere
And sail and talk, and talk and sail,
Until you find Beatrice
Like an endangered species
With luminous antlers
Rising through the Medieval dark.

AESTHETICS OF CAVALCANTI GRIEVING FOR LOST LOVE

Be like a dead person, who seems to those
Who see him a man
Made of branches or stone
Who is able to walk only as a result of cunning
And who has in his heart a wound
Which is, since he is dead,
A visible sign.

AESTHETICS OF CREATING SOMETHING

This doesn't just happen:
It happens to you.

AESTHETICS OF CHINESE OPERA

The Chinese Opera was dealing with what a brain
Has to deal with only part of the time: the excesses and fantasies of kings.

AESTHETICS OF NOAH'S ARK

Every animal needs a mate
Under Ark conditions; its bar is a dark, dull place.

AESTHETICS OF RONSARD

Try to meet
A girl of fourteen
Cassandre Salviati
At Blois
Then never see
Her again
Now write
And write and write
Until you become
An old intellectual bum
Philosopher, esthetician,
Leader of a school,
Monsieur Ronsard
Doctor of the Pléiade.

AESTHETICS OF PAUL KLEE

Little bits of freedom
Imprisoned by light blue sound
Is, it may be, an "oversensitive" way
Of thinking about Paul Klee
For whom smallness relayed a message
To the German-Swiss mountains around.

AESTHETICS OF LORCA

Federico García Lorca stands alone
Luna, typewriter, plantain tree, and dust
The moon is watching him. It is watching over him.

AESTHETICS OF BEING IN HAITI

Don't take off
With a Zombie
On a barge
In the heavy rain.

AESTHETICS OF THE NOVEL

Put one plot
Inside another.

AESTHETICS OF HILL TOWN

Put the cathedral
Or the church
That has the "scheming
Look of an ex-cathedral"
Ronald Firbank's phrase
On top of this hill.

AESTHETICS OF FEELING FINE

Feel fine
Then go away.

AESTHETICS OF DIFFERENCE

What a difference
When the words
Come tangled
In contradictions!

AESTHETICS OF BEING A BOX

Look forward to always containing
What is contained
Whether it is dry
Or raining. Then one morning early
Someone may come by
(This has been known to happen)
Who will take
Your top off! and they will say
Thus, thus! was this result obtained.

AESTHETICS OF OPERA

Don't sing an aria
To someone who can't
Sing one back.

AESTHETICS OF LE GRAND MALENTENDU

Don't be mistaken
About being mistaken—
The Divinities are mistaken time after time

AESTHETICS OF UNION MAN

"You either are a Union man
Or a thug for J. H. Blair"
"I'm working for the Union"

AESTHETICS OF ARISTOTLE

They recognize each other, the one
Who has killed their father, and the other
The one who has killed his son. And she—that woman,
The wife of both—is their sister. They
Are brothers. After twenty years
Unknown to each other, they meet—they
Recognize each other. It is
The Recognition Scene, the
Core of Aristotle's theory
Of the purgative effect of tragedy—he says we feel
The purgative shock effects most
In watching the Recognition Scene.

AESTHETICS OF RIGHT

Right is the aesthetic form
Of good and wrong is the aesthetic form
Of bad. In which case Aesthetics
Is a form (or branch) of Ethics
Which is neither good nor bad.

AESTHETICS OF BEING A ROAD
(Hommage à Rilke)

It is long since you were a lane.
Now you leave off being a street
And don't become a highway yet.
You are cautious
But cautiously exploring what it might be
To be wider than you were before
And go further, and be less familiar with trees.

AESTHETICS OF BEING A MOUSE

Look at the floor.
Look up.
Look at the wall.

AESTHETICS OF POETRY AND PROSE

Chekhov told Bunin
Not to begin writing
Until he felt as cold as ice.
Keats wrote to Shelley
"I am a fever of myself!"

AESTHETICS OF UNANIMITY

The waves come all at once
When you are a sailboat
And the wind
As when you used to be a tree.

AESTHETICS OF FICTION

Don't write stories
That have no plot
And have no characters
And have no style.

AESTHETICS OF INTEGRITY

For every star in the sky
Someone is holding his ground.

AESTHETICS OF EARLY ON

Oh the glove in the fish bowl
Oh the flyers in the sink

AESTHETICS OF HONFLEUR

Put one ship
Next to another
—Honfleur

AESTHETICS OF INSTRUCTION

Do this, do that! is not instruction;
Instruction is a plausible bond
Between one patented enterprise and another.
A song instructs us to be singing;
A house, to live like women and men.

AESTHETICS OF ARIOSTO

Meanwhile someone is going
Another way.

AESTHETICS OF BRANCH

To hang over and to stretch out
To bear leaves
And flowers and fruit—
And still be branching.

AESTHETICS OF ROBERT MUSIL

Musil saw that life
Was without meaning
While at the same time seeing
That Rilke had perfected
Or even that he had discovered
The lyric poem in German.
Before that, it had been nothing
Since the Middle Ages.

Aesthetically one must say
That inside a meaningless whole
Significant particulars exist.
Kicking, passing the ball
And rushing may fill us with life
In even a one-sided game
That is ended by freezing rain.

69

AESTHETICS OF MOSS

Moss covers
Unwilling things
The way old poetry covers
Unwilling subjects:
The death of kings,
Women lost, spring
Arrives, you take
A flower and place it
In your hair or lie
Beside it in the moss.

AESTHETICS OF SAYING GOODBYE
TO A FRIEND

Walk him to the place
Where he can get a taxi
And say good-bye.
If he is wearing
An overcoat
Place one hand
On his shoulder—or if he is not.
Shake hands, embrace
Your friend and say good-bye.
Soon the sky
Will cover him
With only a plane between.

AESTHETICS OF COMEDY
ASLEEP

Don't wake the clown
Or he may knock you down.

AESTHETICS OF CERTAIN THINGS

Certain people for certain things.
Certain women for certain things.
Certain men for certain things.
Certain occasions for certain things.
Certain lives for certain things.

AESTHETICS OF SILENCE

Silence is not everything.
It is half of everything
Like a house.

AESTHETICS OF THE MAIN PART OF LIFE

The late early and the entire middle
Are the main part of life. Be as kind
As you can in this part, and get done
What it seems to you has to be done.
If you find time for it, have a good time.

AESTHETICS OF PLAZA

Christ comes down from the cross
Into a plaza.

AESTHETICS OF OUTDOOR OPERA

Sing as loud
As you can
At the outdoor opera—
It will never
Be loud
Enough.

AESTHETICS OF PENISES

Rising and falling like swans
On Greek vases
Suggesting the connection
To life, that Greek men had,
And satyrs and gods.

AESTHETICS OF CANNON

Being near a cannon
When it was firing
Was as exciting
Stendhal said
As writing
What no one had ever said.

AESTHETICS OF LATE

Light falls on the fountains
When they are off.

AESTHETICS OF THE NUDE

To be a nude
Take off your clothes
And stand
Five or ten feet away
From a painter of nudes.

AESTHETICS OF JAZZ

Play
One
Note
After
Another
On
The
First
Day
Of
The
First
Year
Of
The
First
Century
Of
Jazz.

AESTHETICS OF THE AESTHETICIAN

What is the aesthetician
But a mule hitched to the times?

AESTHETICS OF TALLEYRAND

"No one has any idea
Of the sweetness of life
Who wasn't alive
Before seventeen eighty-nine."

AESTHETICS OF LOUIS KAHN

"The sun never knew
How wonderful it was
Until it fell on the wall
Of a building."

AESTHETICS OF BEAUTY AND DEATH

When one sees a beautiful woman
One can assume that somewhere
(Stendhal says) there is a happy man;
On the other hand,
When one sees a gloomy funeral
One can assume that somewhere
There is a woman or a man
Wondering if going on living is worthwhile.
Put the two together: beautiful woman and gloomy funeral
And what do you get? The death
Of Cleopatra and her obsequies.

AESTHETICS OF SUFFERING

Suffering comes to people as war comes to countries
And issues are clarified. Others are completely lost.

AESTHETICS OF BEING GLORIOUS

To be glorious, take off your wings
Before you fly.

AESTHETICS OF STONE

The gods take stone
And turn it into men and women;
Men and women take gods
And turn them into stone.

AESTHETICS OF PASSING BY *(After Reverdy)*

One shadow—
        Enough!
Is passing by.

A NOTE ABOUT THE AUTHOR

Kenneth Koch lives in New York City and teaches at Columbia University. His books of poetry include *On the Edge, Seasons on Earth, Days and Nights, The Burning Mystery of Anna in 1951, The Art of Love, The Pleasures of Peace, When the Sun Tries to Go On,* and *Thank You.* His short plays, many of them produced off- and off-off-Broadway, are collected in *A Change of Hearts* and *One Thousand Avant-Garde Plays.* He has also published fiction—*The Red Robins* (a novel) and *Hotel Lambosa* (short stories)—and several books on teaching children to write poetry—*Wishes, Lies and Dreams* and *Rose, Where Did You Get That Red?*

A book of selected poems, *On the Great Atlantic Rainway,* is being published at the same time as this volume.

A NOTE ON THE TYPE

The text of this book is set in a film version of *Ehrhardt,* a type face deriving its name from the Ehrhardt type foundry in Frankfurt (Germany). The original design of the face was the work of Nicholas Kis, a Hungarian punch cutter known to have worked in Amsterdam from 1680 to 1689. The modern version of Ehrhardt was cut by The Monotype Corporation of London in 1937.

Composed by Graphic Composition, Inc., Athens, Georgia
Printed and bound by Quebecor Printing, Kingsport, Tennessee
Designed by Harry Ford